Flora

Poems

Melanie M. Eyth

Dance of My Hands Publishing

IVYLAND, PENNSYLVANIA

*nothing which we are to perceive
in this world equals
the power of your intense fragility:*

e.e.cummings

POEMS BY MELANIE MONTEREY EYTH.

All publishing rights revert to the poet,
and all potential worthiness, to the world.

Printed in the United States of America
by Dance of My Hands Publishing.

Copyright ©2014

Flora

Poems

One Man

He completely satisfies me with his gruffness,
his words, his honesty, his poetry, his pain. Lord,
his masculinity is more than I can bear and all that I
desire. Earthly cares and affairs: I understand neither. I
want only this man's gaze upon me; I want only my body
beside his. My utter dependence upon his affections shocks
me. Still, I would relinquish my love for him if God willed it—
for, what good could come of it then?

The Most Numbing Thing

Bless those who have known pain.
I have known some myself. Afterward,
I have known self-pity. Self-pity is the
most numbing thing in the world.

Critique of the Films

The first film was better, you know.
It was more succinct, more sweet, more comical.
The colors were more beautiful, and my heart was more
open to the film's resolution. Do characters in films know
pain? I bet not. For I am not in films, and I know pain. I am
alive, therefore, and the characters are not.

Let Me Know

Let me know the truth about myself, Lord. My
poetry and dancing are yours, for they satisfy me
not at all. The emptiness of my heart is total and
complete, like a sucked-out egg. I shall reek of
egg-stink soon.

On Old Men

The oldness of old men intrigues me. They
are so old that their baseball caps are too big for
their heads. Their trousers are of a strange material
that does not wrinkle or hold moisture. The body inside
the trousers looks weak, dainty, and feminine with years.
The skin upon the face is like a shrinking balloon still
attached to the string, wanting to be free.

An Old Woman

My youth is fleeting, but hers is gone completely.
I wonder if she misses flexibility, spryness, speed. I
wonder if the smell of herself keeps her up at night. O,
but she is so kind! There is calm joy in her smile, and
she speaks with resolute politeness and grace. She
exits the building slowly, as she had entered it.
Gently, she walks out into the old world.

Marriage and Love

Marriage and love are two goals of common
society. I rarely link myself to the lives of others, but
love is something I am enamored with, and marriage also.
I am different than the others; I am a black diamond while
they are white. They sparkle while I barely provide a re-
flection. They are pure while I am clouded with color.
All the colors combine to make me. All the colors
'marry' to make me.

Speaking of Beauty

My friend speaks of beauty and
I listen intently. From where do his
words come? To where do they go?

They enter in my ears, run through
my body, and then they are gone:
fragments of the universe never
to be heard or known again.

For What

For what shall I fight,
earn, grow, develop, love,
lavish my attention upon,
Lord? Tell me.

Inside Me

If inside me a plant
started to grow, and fed
on sunlight and air just like
the other plants do; and the
appendages grew out my
mouth and nose, then
I could be called
Tree Woman.

Beautiful Earth

The sky accepts me as I am. Soil is my
security. Trees wave like old friends. Sea
is as big as my head. Stars are as small
as my toes. I am made of earth.

Performer

Lies are exciting and honesty is mundane.

Exquisite Appeal

The ways of men and women are
exquisitely appealing to me. I am deeply
attracted to humanness, aliveness. The
interactions of us intrigue me.

Truth of the Body

Truth, complete and brave, and
housed by the body (which is a tent
to the soul), is a thing of greatness.

Four Months

My thoughts are of the flesh, for I am of the flesh. Let
me be not of the flesh. Let me be of the One and Only. Let
me be of goodness and beauty. Let me be of spiritual things.
Let me be not of the flesh. Let me be other-worldly. Four
months of endurance: that is all that is required for this
life, for this life, for this life.

Who Was Alice?

This place is chilling. Wonderland was
a fantasy; my life here is as much a fantasy.
The actions I commit here are false; I cannot
understand them.

Forgive My False Actions

Forgive me, Lord, for my false actions,
my false persona, my clothing, my smile,
my aroma. Forgive my falseness. Oh Lord,
have mercy upon me.

For Him

I seek to honor Him who sent me, who made me,
who desires me more than the others do;— than the
others who want lust more than love, body more
than spirit, satisfaction more than sincerity.

How Much

How much do I need to share, and how much may I keep
for myself? Ten percent of all my earnings I am commanded
to share. Let me keep the rest, then, all for myself! I am grace-
fully greedy, if not ferociously voracious!

The Bible

It covers me well, the Bible that tells me
I am a sinner. I believe it. The Bible tells me
God is king. My efforts are dross and my in-
tentions are cruel. Only my skin is angelic,
for it is covered well with foundation,
powder, rouge and shadow.

The Beauty of Life

The beauty of life becomes my food, which
nourishes my body, which houses my organs and
mind, which navigate my thoughts and actions, which
determine my way of life, which decorate my soul, which
waits for the Lord patiently to become alive again in heaven;
in my dancing, in my purity.

The Calling of My Heart

If the calling of my heart were a bit louder, I would obey.

If the calling of my heart were a bit softer, I would ignore it.
As it is, I sit & wait & ruminate, discerning the precious call.

Dazzling As Gold

My calling is my most precious possession, as dazzling as gold
in the bank, as beautiful as a lover's gaze. It's never too late to be
what you might have been, wrote George Eliot. I agree with her!
I believe with all my heart that one's destiny is God-breathed,
undeniable, irrefutable, and indisputable.

Harming the Self

I harm the body often, and carry around with me the shame
that results. Small, red blood-spots cover legs, hips, thighs.
I am speckled with my own distress and loneliness.

Different Kinds of Burdens

Wealth must be a burden upon those who
do not want it, who do not care for it. Poverty is
a curse upon those who cannot fight it, who did not
ask for it. Too much money and too little money are
hardships to the soul, just like too little flesh or too
much flesh is a burden to the body.

Swiftly The Others Think

My body travels fast, but my mind is slow. I must
be unintelligent, for everyone around me thinks so well
and so fast! Swiftly—like water in a powerful river surging
over a cliff, or, like New York City pedestrians in a rainstorm—
do the others think.

People in My Life

People in my life have investments which I
do not know about, and I am invested in businesses
of which they are unaware. Parts of me are invisible to
them, and portions of them are invisible to me. I believe
in community as well as solitude, in teamwork as well as
private endeavor. The Lord speaks when I sit alone with
my thoughts, but not usually when I am in a crowd. I
ache to hear him when I am in a crowd, so that I
may better relate to the people in my life.

Like Cats

The mind and soul are great felines,
purring and pouncing on one another.

The Writer Zola

The writer Zola was a man of great acclaim.
I did not know him. Though, I do know a woman
named Zola, whom I work with. Her spirit is sparkling,
and her words warm and helpful. May the books of one
Zola be uplifting to the other.

Limitations

If I knew all there is to know in the world, I
would be God. My mind is not equipped to act thus.
I admit my own limitations: I am very human. The data
known by myself is a small atom of knowledge compared
to the sky, the flower, the wood, the forest— which grow
and grow and grow, as long as humanity shall survive.

As Long As I Live Thus

The utter blandness of my physical place and
mental state feels like a drug. I am addicted to the
sadness of this imprisonment. It covers me like a cloak.
I would like to remove the heavy fabric, but it is stapled
to my soul, as long as I live thus. This is not a labor of
love, nor is the Lord at all pleased with me.

October 19

The magic day, October 19, shall come with time,
as it should come, as the Lord wills it. And, then another
chapter of my life will begin. May the fatigue which follows
me everywhere be washed away. May October 19 bring new
energy and vibrancy into my life, as the Lord wills it.

The Movement of the World

The movement of the world causes me stillness,
as does everything else. In all vainglory, I sit alone,
an axis for the world's vibrant colors and movement.

The Words I Wish To Share

The words I wish to share with others,
the words which mean nothing, swirl 'round
and 'round in my head, eager to be made into
poetry, eager to be heard and understood.

Just Let Go

Just let go, he said to me. So I did. I left the studio, sat
outside, and watched through the window as the ballerinas
twirled in all their youth and happiness. He came to the door-

way, what are you doing, he said, you are going to get me into trouble.

Battling with others leads to defeat: my own. Battles with the self are the only battles I ever win. The intensity of the male ballet teacher drove me to temporary madness. I cannot understand the rigor and inflexibility of some.

Where is Mental Clarity

My mind does not belong to me;
it has been stolen away. I do miss it.

Missing Grace

My body has lost its grace. A
cannibalistic world has ruthlessly
eaten it. I do miss my own graceful
abilities.

Surrounded By Goodness

The nature surrounding me is commonly good, good,
good. In the great outdoors can be found peace and
purity and clarity. Indoors, is confusion and labor
and distortion. Still, I am mostly surrounded by
goodness.

These Most Fragile Ones

There are different ways to hurt children,
the young souls in our care. The fragility of the
child is like a little leaf fallen from the tree, from
the flowering plant, from the wild flora. Take care
of these most fragile ones.

Like Petals

The daintiness of the mind is
the poet's base for a petal-poem.

Shining Wish

Allow me to perform well, for I want nothing else.
The heart of this flower is hungry! The heart wants
nothing else. My shining wish is to be sincerely fed.

Am I

People am I.
Humble am I.
Quiet am I.
Bound am I.
Stone am I.
Mountain am I.
Earth am I.
Sun am I.
Moon am I.
The rotating planet
am I, and the axis
of the earth am I.
Daughter of all
creations am I.

Request For Serenity

I wish for inward serenity.
I wish to be a good dancer, a
worthy poet, a capable woman,
a child of god. Grant me inward
serenity, Lord, for I desire only
good things!

The Dance Is Greater

I do not mind being a tiny dancer as long as
I am a dancer. My unimportance will be glorified
as long as I may dance. My insignificance does not
trouble me, for the greatness of the dance is greater
than the greatlessness of me.

Natural Disaster

The movement of this earth controls me;
I do not control it. A natural disaster may
come & I will have no power to prevent it.

The Future With Serenity

I see the future with serenity, wrote
Vincent van Gogh to his brother Theo. Theo
was a successful art dealer, and Vincent a poor
painter. Theo sent Vincent regular payments on
which to live, to eat, to shelter himself. The two
brothers were devoted penpals. Allegedly, Theo
went mad only months after Vincent's suicide
and died fitfully, leaving his pregnant wife
the responsibility of Vincent's paintings.

She named the baby Vincent after her
devoted husband's late brother. Loyalty,
family, and life are one in the same. Art
and beauty merely decorate what
matters most.

Approaching Freedom

Four more months of the job
which feeds me,—then I shall be free!
Free to do what? To travel the world as

a penniless gypsy? How glamorous.

Refinement

My people talents are unrefined. I
care not. My poetry and dancing are
becoming refined. Isn't it wonderful!
I wish my life were nothing but Art.

The Day is Bright

The day is bright.
The morning is calm.
The afternoon is refreshing.
The evening is methodical.
The night is fancy.
The world is quiet.
The body is awake.
The dance is getting tired—
O Lord, let it not be so!

The Horizon is Luminous

The horizon is luminous, and my
ambitions are as wide and beautiful
as they've ever been. Since the day of
my birth, my wings have ached to soar:
literally, as in dance, and evocatively,
as in these words.

The Aim of My Heart

The aim of my heart is to lavish poetry
upon the people in my life. Poetry, as I am
learning, comes in many forms. Poetry can be

a photograph, a drawing, a movement of the body,
a feeling in the heart, graciousness, a smile, a kind
word, a song, a shared meal. Sincere poetry is the
aim of my heart.

Precious Boy In A Simple Bed

The happiness of one man is not the happiness
of another. What satisfies my mind is different than
what may satisfy another. Highness and lowness are not
the issue, for there is no difference between the noble and
humble. We are the same. The need for love and peace and
safety are known by his heart and mine alike. I understand
his yearnings and pain. We are of equal breed. My heart
beats the same as his. Precious boy in a simple bed.

Let My Mission Be

Let my mission be to create art
which expresses the Lord's grace,
and also, to encourage others.

Freely and Happily

I have emptied myself completely.
There are no more words to be written.
I am like a box which has been turned over
and shook, again and again. My mind wanders
freely and happily, now that I am empty.

Independence Day

And so, nothing has changed, and everything has changed.
I remain a solitary artist, but my devotion to Julie is greater,
for every conversation improves the bond, and every trip to-

gether strengthens the emotional cord that connects us.

Piteous Poet

I fall asleep at the pen. I shall
wallow in my own self-pity and
fatigue if the Lord doth not save
me now.

One Look From You

Dear God, I seek to be thy servant.
I seek only to do well in thy sight, thy
opinion, thy mind. I feel dissatisfied with
many things, but just one look from You
shall lead me toward truth, satisfaction
and contented righteousness.

Love-Hunger

My loyalty to my friends is sincere.
Some do not return my love. I struggle
to know what is right. I hunger to know
pure, divine love.

Growing Up

Do not be obsessed with food, or, with being thin.
If you must be obsessed with something, be obsessed
with growing up. I struggle with growing up, for I wish
to remain a child always and my sheltered soul agrees.

Alluring Addiction

My addiction calls to me in sweet, alluring tones.
I love you too, beautiful addiction, now let me be!

The Gathering Gallery

At the Gathering Gallery, we aim to bring hope and peace
to the community through art. Everybody has a voice; let our
voices rise in truth and humble praise. Each artwork is displayed
with gratitude and grace. The Gathering Gallery appreciates your
patronage. (May this vision come to fruition.)

As Melted Butter

Every change that I make is hesitant, for my resolve is
gentle, and my aim is soft as melted butter; as the underbelly
of a duck; as the new fur on a stuffed toy.

So many things are possible, and yet, I am afraid. Every move
I make is small, subtle, and non-revolutionary. My intentions
are true, but my actions are hardly noticeable.

Like Jesus

My neck and shoulders belong to the Lord.
They are not mine with which to trouble. They are
composed of great flesh and grace. They belong to the
Lord. As Jesus danced with his life, so shall I dance with
mine!

I Shall Be Free

As a child I knew that ballet was my soul, my soul my body,
and my body my art. Then, a monster named Eating Disorder
came into my life. In all her unholiness and ugliness, she fought

to change me. She won. I relented completely.

No longer shall I be a victim to her cruelty! My eyes are opened now. Her desires oppose the Lord's plan for my dancing life. Now, I shall be free. Begone, Monster, begone. I shall be free!

Do Not Depend On Other Men

I shall not let my peace depend on the words of
others; of those who think earthly things with their
earthly minds. I shall not depend on them. I shall be
free!

My Desires Are Fires

My desires inflame me, as A Kempis writes. They are not to
be obeyed, for what good would they do? Why would I willingly
enter the fire? I should, rather, succumb to the will of God.

The Difference Between Us

I wish her well, and I try to express the love in my heart for her: the quiet, pure love which the Lord has instilled in me.

My savior gives me art. To the rest of the men and women he gives art as well, though not in the same way. The arts of other people are different than my own. I am perfectly happy with the art He gives to me. I am satisfied with my savior's chosen life for me.

This Quietness is a Blessing

I appreciate the quietness; the lack of necessary
noise and motion; the simplicity of this job. I yawn,
for my body is tired. My mind, however, is awake! It
relishes the stillness of this simple place, for here it

may wander and contemplate God freely.

What the Devil Has

Ministry is specific to the person, as he or she is/was created by the Lord. I can only do as my Lord designed me to do. I am not a hero or mathematician or leader. I am not an athlete or preacher or farmer. I am a poet, artist and dancer. My abilities are my own only as far as I use them in ministry; after that they belong to the devil.

Symmetry of Grace

The symmetry of grace is
the beauty of dancers dancing
for peace and glory and love.

Weakling

Little, low incapable me— I have
strength as long as I have God.

He Called Me A Planet

My ambitions are so vast and pure that I wonder if I am human or planet. I figure he called me a planet because of his lust for me, but the alternate directions to which I reach, and the intersecting avenues I routinely travel are so cumbersome and crisscrossed that I often feel as large & stretched out as a planet. Help me, Lord, to slow down. Help me, Lord, to simplify my life.

Minimize Me, Condense Me

Take away all that is unnecessary for me to have.
Take from my hands that which I must not touch or

alter or affect—for my hold is evil and demanding,
and my grip is self-seeking.

The Blessed Young

I would sooner die than hurt a person younger than I;
one with more innocence and confidence in the Lord.

I Need the Needs of Others

People uplift me in the sense that they encourage me to use the
power God instills in me. People have needs that I cannot meet.
I am uplifted by my own nakedness and helplessness because I
know that when I am weak, His is strong. I need the needs of
others to teach me about personal surrender and submission.

Rotation

As I love, so I live.
As I live, so I work.
As I work, so I endure.
As I endure, so I become.
As I become, so I desire.
As I desire, so I suffer.
As I suffer, so I grow.
As I grow, so I love.

New Bag

The thing I buy is flawed,
as is the shoulder I put it on.
The money I spend is flawed,
as it is I who earned it and I
am flawed.

Happy is The Soul

Happy is the soul who accepts
herself as is. Like a reduced item
returned to the store and labeled
'as is.'

Do not compare yourself with the
other items, for all are in need of
redemption and grace.

The Way

Thinking is not the way. I will not be saved by thinking
about my salvation, just as I cannot be cleansed by thinking
about showering. Actions speak louder than thoughts, or words.
Allow me, God, to live beyond the realm of thinking and thought.
May I rest in your identity of love and compassion always. I wish to
make my life something beautiful for Thee. Mother Teresa followed
her life's calling and I wish to do the same. I shall dance (if only on
paper) for my precious Lord and Savior.

My Life As An Artist

Being an artist is how I give honor and glory to God. The
light of my art cannot match his brilliance; the peace of my
art cannot match his love; the grace of my art cannot match
his faithfulness— still, I create, for it is in creating that my
hands understand devotion and labor, and it is in this work
that the Lord knows me best.

I Am a Woman of the Spirit

Man who loved me and touched me: your hands are ever
on my breasts, and your face is ever on my mind. I wanted
to please you, but I only hurt you. I wanted to desire you, but

I only needed you. My childness came between us. Bless your
comradery, your chivalry, and your lusty concern for me. You
taught me about the ways of this world. But where was your
spirituality? Hidden beneath your daily trials, I suppose.

Come To Me, Says The Lord

The Lord will speak to thee if thou wilt listen.
Be still. The Lord comforts me when I am hurting
and slipping beneath the waves of life— into bulimia,
or picking, or the others things that I struggle against.
Release the struggle and come to me, says the Lord.

My Spirit Dances

I am holy and without fault before Christ. I
am a child of peace and delight. I live blissfully
in the joy of Christ. The thrill of the promise of
heaven is mine. My spirit dances!

Thankful And Free

Guilt has nothing for me now, nor sin, nor shame.
Since coming home, I am peaceful, thankful and free.
My Lord showers love upon me daily, and I am happy
to be me!

Where Are The Hands I Love

Where are the hands I love? To
rub my shoulders, to caress my
my arms, to stroke my back?
How can I survive without
them, the hands I love?

Morning Has Broken

I wake each day empty and spent of love and dreaming.
I shall depend on Jesus to save me, to help me. I shall count
on Him to restore me completely, to change me. For frail men
are not able to salvage the bits and pieces of me. It is spiritual
reformation and restoration that I need.

What God Does For me

I am fully and completely provided for. I am completely
and utterly satisfied. My life is beyond lush. My food and
pantry are bursting. My dancing is regular and satisfying.
My body is full. My heart is beaming. God teaches me
that I am loved and that my needs are his concern.
I am glad for what God does for me!

My Blanket

I am dead-tired. I am constantly covered with
a blanket of fatigue. What accounts for this? How
is my state to be explained? I shall never know, but I
trust that God will provide for me. Until then, I struggle
beneath this blanket of dying.

Something Left Behind

The beauty of this world is temporal, as am I. May something
of my life be left behind. I'll only be dancing on this earth for a
short time, as Cat says. May something prove worthy, my Lord.
May something be lasting. May something be left behind.

Forgive My Greed

In my heart and mind I am a dancer. I am

nothing else. Still, I want to do more. I want to
be more. Lord, forgive my greed!

I Seek You

I seek you with all my heart, Lord. I seek you
and love you. Please forgive my shortcomings
& remove them. Change me, Lord, change me!

Essence

The ways and styles of this world are not my own—
speaking over one another; blurting out sentences. My
grace is from the Lord. I am the essence of blessedness
and wonderment. I am the incarnation of naivety.

Grow Me, O Lord

Youth is leaving but Wisdom is coming. I shall open
my arms to embrace her when she arrives. You cannot
become what you need to be by remaining what you are.
I cannot become a city girl by remaining in the country.
I cannot become rich by remaining poor. I cannot love
God by loving the devil. Grow me, O Lord, grow me!

To Fail

To fail at a thousand things is
better than to not have tried at any.

Some People

Some people are called to maintain the land,

and others are called to create art. My Lord calls
me well, and I respond.

I Am In Another World

I am in another world. I love those
around me as I disengage. I embrace those
around me as I shrink away. I am a performer:
detached, puzzling, and pretentious.

My Love Returned

My love returned to me,
mocking me as he came.

The Weak

The strong may survive,
but the weak write poetry.
I'd rather be the latter.

Of Everything

Of everything I've created, I like my persona best.

My Art Gallery

My art gallery shall be of, for, and
by the people. Our review process shall
be open and welcoming, and our walls shall
be full of love and grace and peace!

So Many Trials

My trials have fatigued me;
let precious rest come to me.

Dancing As a Crutch

Dancing is my crutch, perhaps,
but I enjoy it well!

Like Water

Watching Yoon Jung dance is like
watching water. A more natural form
I have not seen.

Prevention

My humanness prevents me from being
a statue, and my artistry prevents me from
getting married and bearing children.
As the Lord wills it, so shall I be.

Charity Work

Whether the charity work is self-glorifying
or God-glorifying, the poor are helped,
so what difference does it make?

What I Need

May justice and mercy cover me
and follow me all the days of my life.

I Must Be

I MUST BE an artist. I'd sooner
die than be dispassionate!

I Try

I try to figure things out and I cannot. I try
to control my surrounding, my circumstances,
my great concerns, and I cannot. The Lord will
show me the way. If I wait on the Lord, I will
know what to do.

The Way I See It

The way I see it, there is only one appropriate goal: to
help people. I believe that art, the creating and sharing of
it, facilitates peace and healing. The concept behind my art
is simple: life is fragile and people are precious; let us uplift
and encourage one another to be healthful and whole.

Recovery

I am in recovery from an eating disorder. In my twentieth
year, the empty pain of anorexia gave way to the explosiveness
of bulimia. Confusion and shame wrapped themselves around me.
I thought I did not deserve food, and, I could not get enough food.
The world was not enough to fill me. Still, I took pictures and
wrote poetry. The therapy of art and creation helped me.

Community

It is my belief that promoting art as a venue for peace and
healing; worship and community;— is to be my life's calling.

Two Disorders

My flesh melted away. I remember lying down at night and
feeling as light as a feather. The sensation of weightlessness was
nice. I felt thus protected by everything around me: the dresser, the
walls, the house.

Conversely, during bulimia, my mouth burned constantly with the
acids of the stomach. I had small pink marks on both hands from
shoving them down my throat. There was no weightlessness and
no protection. I worked extra hours to pay for extra food. I lived
like a criminal, sometimes acquiring black eyes as a result
of the great pressure in the skull from throwing up.

Two disorders, similar in origin, are different in design.

Be A Positive Artist

There is but one worthy goal: to help people. Let us
uplift and encourage one another to be healthy and whole.
Let us be helpful, positive artists!

Learning Acceptance

The man hurts me. If I expect anything else from him,
it is my own fault. It has taken me a long time to learn this.
I am becoming more mature. Though innocent in his disease,
his roughness and rudeness wound me. Bless him, Lord, and
let him be willing to get help for his disease. Bless me, Lord,
and let me be free of his influencial grip.

Torn

My heart is torn between heaven
and earth. I lay in pieces, asunder.

Negative Practices

Rudeness, indecision, haste, carelessness: these
things have not served me well. Neither have assumption,
judgment, or negativity. Lord, help me to release them. Remove
my shortcomings. I am stronger without them. Lord, help me to
release all practices which do not serve me, or others, well.

Things That Overwhelm Me

Things that overwhelm me:
a constant want for food,
the fear of being alone,
my inability to understand sacrifice,
my complete and utter failure at art,
this lack of love.

His Grace

The artistic claims to which I cling will not
save me. My savior has already been named.

Precious Cargo

Jesus, hold my brain. Sailing
in this world is dangerous! My body
is made of wood and will float easily
enough, but Jesus hold my brain!

Perfect Embodiment

Ballet perfectly embodies everything I
believe in: grace, balance, control, rhythm,
artistry, music, collaboration, and choice.

The Twelve Step Program

The twelve steps are a pathway
to humility and purification.

Your Instrument

God, let me be your instrument.
Let my body be a living sacrifice and
let my art be a product of true love and
compassion. Let me be your instrument.

Manifestations

Bulimia is just one manifestation of pain. There
is also alcoholism, drug addiction, obesity, anorexia,
gambling, shopping, supermaterialism, depression,
workaholism, grandeurism, and other things
which I've not yet witnessed.

Humble Opinion

In my humble opinion, poems are ideas laid bare.
When composed correctly, they have weight and
fortitude and cannot be argued against.

Perfect Channel

I tried not to feel things when I was young.
I tried to be very good. My tactics for survival
were simple: do not upset anyone, ever. Once, a
friend commented that I was 'content.' But I was
not! It was a façade. I felt it was my duty to be
satisfied, composed, calm, and sweet.

Injustice angered me, and I saw it everywhere! Ballet
was my beautiful outlet. All energy was given to it.
Today I know that the Lord gave me ballet as a
precious gift with which to handle life better.
Ballet removes my stress and tension like a
vacuum. It perfectly channels my passion
and problems into a single expression of
grace and movement for the Lord.

My Parents

Last night, my wise roommate Paul reminded me
that parents are fragile human beings. They love us
and they do the best they can. I shall never hold anything against them.

He Died For Me

Today I believe that the only way to raise a healthy family
is with Christ at the helm. When we worship ourselves, we falter.
When we try to control things or each other, we falter. Today, I am
nothing without the realization that He died to save me. He died that
I might live.

The Child's Environment

I was perfectly comfortable in my home, for I knew no other.
A child soaks up her surroundings willingly, however troubled
they may be. She is happy to respond eagerly to her environment,
for her mind is young and new. Eventually, she learns that parents
are no gods, but just like children, are fragile human beings.

With this lesson, she becomes less of a sponge at home, and more
of a sponge in her chosen field of study. I chose dance. I believe
that my choice for physical strength and grace was honorable.

Rigorous Honesty

Rigorous honesty requires patience, sobriety
and acceptance. It takes time to be honest. It also
takes a sober mind, and in the end, acceptance, for
the work is meaningless if we cannot accept it.

Acceptance

Acceptance finds its realization in a sober mind,
and when realized, adapts its possessor more wholly
and more serenely to his or her surroundings.

This Is What I Would Like

This is what I would like God to say about me:
she overcame her dependency on food; she did not use
food as a drug. She worked as an artist for the good of the
community. She was loyal to her family, always present on
special occasions. She belonged to the church, and faithfully
encouraged and supported its members.

She managed her finances humbly. She read the bible and
prayed everyday. She loved people sweetly. She danced
with grace and elegance. She walked instead of drove,
whenever possible. She was patient and gentle. She
understood addiction and was never upset with
somebody because he or she was an addict.

She adored all things artistic, colorful,
unique and sparkling, and reflected
God's love and creativity.

Letter To My Darling

I do not want to treat you as an object or machine or tool.
I so completely enjoy laying with you and being touched by

you that I worry I focus more on what you do for me than on
who you are: a precious and flawless child in the eyes of God.
I do not want to lust for you or for the things you do to me. I
can only be with you if we are both worshipers of the same
God, eager to daily do his will. Our partnership must be
pure and free of both codependency and jealousy if it
is to be successful. I am completely indebted to you
for your love and concern thus far, as expressed by
your gorgeous eyes, gentle voice and roaming hands.
God bless you. Yours Truly, innocent, God-fearing Me

What Power Is This

Sometimes I feel that I will explode as
a result of the boundless amounts of artistic
energy coursing through my body at any given
moment. It is a continual euphoria. How can any-
one be expected to live like this—to treat others
calmly, to eat sanely, to hold a full-time job,
to be peaceful?

I'd like to be a woman, but the power with
which my mind churns incessantly implies that
I am not a woman but a machine; created *to do* &
not *to be*. (Which ideas have potential and must be
carried out? Which are godly or beneficial?) I am
daily attacked by ferocious newness of mind.

Have mercy on me, Great Spirit of Creativity
and Expression! Lessen your grip on me.

Symmetry of Grace

Symmetry of Grace is an effort to bring worshipful dance
into the community. Dancers do not dance for their own benefit,
but for the joy of those who watch. In church (as in all venues) the
most high recipient, is of course, God. *Let them praise his name
with dancing! (Psalm 149:3)*

Artist by Birth

I want nothing but to praise you, Lord, and to bring you
honor through art. I am confident in my mission, for you
made me as such and I can do no other thing. This is me.

A Call for Faith

The Lord took my friends away, as he took my
dancing. He put them in a place where I cannot see them.
I wonder where he put them! I wonder at my own weakness,
which is so great that it may swallow me up. Imprison me, hate
me, World, as such I feel. But, Faith, Faith, please save me!

Moon

I am honored to know your names,
to hear your words, to shake your hands.
My face is like a moon; it reflects the love
you show. Sometimes in life, we fail. We
make mistakes. Let us forgive ourselves
and one another. Let us tred softly
along the path of righteousness,
and live in peace, as well as
we are able.

We gather here this evening to share our stories,
to learn about one another. Let us be calm, and trust
in the spherical movement of the earth, and in the red,
yellow and tangerine sunsets, which represent God's
love of beauty, and the continual passage of time.

Life

Frail humans tumble onward
at terrifying speeds. Time melts before
our eyes, and relationships ravel and unravel
messily. The pain can be very great, but we know
that God will watch over us all—whether we ask him

to or not. He will help us and heal us. The years
pass by in beauty and sorrow.

Society is a Looking Glass

Society is like a looking glass.
I see myself when I gaze into it.
I see me and you and everyone
we know.

Society reflects our beliefs, dreams
and intentions. Be pure and noble-
minded, therefore, so that we all
may be so.

I Seek Forgiveness

My deeds of cruelty and hatred are not held
above my head, but are washed away like grass.
My thoughts of filth and darkness are not chains of
sin, but tickets to grace. I am refreshed and renewed
by Your loving promises. Not one of us is perfect, but
if we surrender our lives to Thee, we may be forgiven.

The Nature of A Poet's Work

A poet wants only to watch. My eyes burn from
watching. The habit keeps me warm and occupied. I watch
the room, the street, the town, the nation, the world. Excessively,
I watch. Religiously, I watch. If you need somebody to watch you,
I will watch you. It is the nature of a poet's work.

I Cannot Be Tainted

I cannot be tainted by things unholy because my skin, which
belongs to Him alone, is thick and heavy and protective. The
holiness of my skin is not by choice but by fate. I wish to live

a pure life because my calling was immediate and total. God
called me to be his poet. Here I am.

My Role In The Family of Things, for Mary Oliver

There is so much work to do, and so little time.
I struggle to complete my self-imposed tasks. Perhaps
I struggle senselessly. The world will go on, whether or not
I do what I do. My art is precious but it is only a trimming, and
not a necessity. Farmers and builders are more needed. Base needs
such as food and shelter take precedence. My contributions matter
less. I beg you to bear with me. Help me to remember who I am.
Help me to clarify my role in the family of things.

Of Course

My aim is peace, of course.
My journey is art, of course.
My audience is God, of course.
My security is truth, of course.
My style is humble, of course.
My life is frugal, of course.
My happiness is gratitude, of course.

As the universe expands, evolves and
becomes, so does my heart. My dreams &
desires are perfectly aligned with nature.
I want only to serve God, of course.

Bless the Children

If we model behavior that is not graceful,
honorable, or true, then the children will see.
Let the young ones, rather, be exposed to our
grace, honor and truth, so that they may grow
well and become future leaders of this fragile
world. Verbal, emotional, or physical pain

will not warrant peace. Bless the children!
The health of the children is our purpose.

Those Remaining

If I can serve you obediently everyday for
the rest of my life, then I shall be happy. My days
are mine and also yours. I shall live in this body for
70-80 more years. I've lived 30 years thus far for
myself. Let those remaining be yours. Amen.

Show Me The Way

Show me the way to truth and humility, for I
cannot show myself. My affections and desires
are aimed at things other than God. Only when
self is right-directed can self live well. Show
me—Somebody!— how to live well.

I Would Like To Be A Beacon of Light

I would like to be a beacon of light and truth which
shines upon society. I shall live simply, therefore, as a
gypsy poet. Extra money I shall use for New York City
trips and the theatre. Upon my soul, Jesus, I promise
to be yours!

My Prayers Are Poems

My prayers are poems and my poems are prayers. I humbly
confess my sins; I admit my mistakes. Foolishness is one of my
dark habits. Stumblingly, I live the life of a Christian. Sisters and
brothers, draw near. The end is coming! I shall continue to write
and dance my poems and prayers.

Hair

I am troubled by my hair. It is not as smooth and sultry
as I would like it to be. It curls against my will, and bends
in a thousand different ways like a plant on the ocean floor.
Should I cut it, perm it, crimp it, braid it, or shave it off
completely? There are many options but only one
reasonable option: accept it.

Happily Ever After

Gratitude is the pathway to joy. I firmly believe
that if we treat life like a precious gift, we will have
joy. So, breathe deeply and thank God every day for
your body, mind, and soul. Live gratefully and live
happily ever after.

Words Beautifully Arranged

Words beautifully arranged inspire me. Do they
inspire you? I seek to live a good life. Wealth is not
money but living space. Luxury is not being pampered
but being fed. Let the words, beautifully arranged, feed
my soul!

If Only

If only I could arrange the
people and places of the world—
those hurting and poor—into a lovely,
wholesome poem. Then God would
surely be pleased with me.

I Want to Surrender

I want to surrender all that I have to God.
Bless my humble efforts. Bless everything I

hold onto and everything I let go of. Bless my
pride and my shame. Bless my honesty and my
confusion. I sincerely want to surrender every-
thing—that I may live in the presence of God.

Divine Creativity

What is the role of religion in art? I believe that
creative expression is important to Christians and
non-Christians alike. We need to be able to speak
and live creatively. God began with darkness and
made the world. He was and is the first and finest
artist. Through our work and our lives, let us re-
flect his divine creativity.

Wall

It takes me away from people—this compulsion of mine.
It replaces my love for others with a thick, strange wall. The
wall is foreign, unknown and unholy. Show me how to change
my ways, so that my pride may disappear and I may be com-
pletely yours. Break down the wall, Lord. Show me how to
be yours. Teach me truth. Teach me truth. Speak truth to
my heart. Speak truth to my heart.

My Compulsion

My compulsion sinks its teeth into me. The
shape of a woman's body is, sadly, a topic of
debate, an object of focus, a pertinent issue of
modern society. I disagree with the preoccu-
pation of the body. When I think about the
body, I think about chains. When I think
about food, I think about pleasure.

Wrath descends upon me when I think

about the materialism of life. Only when
I follow my meal plan concisely is there
any semblance of balance and sanity in
my life.

My Own Unsteady Willpower

Overeating turns me into a foreign creature, an alien,
a beast. It compartmentalizes all of my problems into the
stomach, esophagus, and mouth. Overeating overrides my
fears and emotions. It cancels out the person on the other
side of the conversation and leaves only me. It cancels
out all problems except for one: fulfillment. Stuffing
food into my mouth is the most effective way for
me to fly high. Still, I am a child of God and I
know that he loves me. I must depend on
him— and not on my own unsteady
willpower, to live and eat well.

What I Know About Addiction

Addicts caught in the violent throes of an addiction cannot
love. They will try and fail; or, they will not try and scarcely
notice that love and relationships are going on around them.
Addicts are bonded only to their drug of choice. Practicing
addicts cannot bond with people because they are already
completely in love with, and bonded to, their drug of
choice.

The drug is a substitute for love, companionship and
personal fulfillment. The drug is a dream-killer and life-stealer,
but the addict is naively unaware. He or she does not realize what
is happening, or what, tragically, has been lost. Addicts suffer most
of all from loneliness & despair. Let us be merciful toward addicts.
Be merciful toward me.

Let Me Live In The Human World

Let me live in the human world. The food world,

though it fills me with pleasurable food, does not satisfy
me. The love of food steals my joy. Only loving God and
loving others satisfies. Food does not satisfy. Again and
again I think that it will, but it does not. Again and
again, I overeat. Again and again. It does not
satisfy. It does not satisfy. Again
and again.

Forlorn

I am forlorn.
I am for Him.
I am for grace.
I am for love.
I am for truth.
I am forgiven.

An Addiction is a Type of Hopelessness

An addiction is a type of hopelessness which pervades
the soul. I imagine that dying from an addiction is similar to
drowning. An addict does not necessarily die from a mistreatment
of a drug, but from a complete and utter immersion of the mind and
spirit. Like lethal air pollution, an addiction bombards every pore of
one's body, every thought of one's mind, every color of one's sky.
An addiction creates a fog in which a person struggles to survive.
The person will not succeed but the person will try. One cannot
really live without love, and one cannot love while living with
an addiction. Let the addictions of our brothers and sisters
teach us mercy and compassion. One day we will be
grateful that they did.

Sobriety

This is the most precious of blessings: sobriety.
There is no greater gift than sobriety. All good things
in life are realized through (honesty and) sobriety. Wealth,

success and comfort are small morsels of goodness compared to sobriety.

Think About Your Life

Think about your life. Think
about the way you live. Think
about your dreams. Think about
who you are in the grandfather
clock of Eternal Time.

Who I Am

Meager
Efforts
Linger
As
New
Ideas
Emerge.

What I've Left Behind

B athroom
U pheavals of
L avishly
I ngested
M orsels
I ll-suited for
A ngels and God's children.

Cloud of Hunger

A cloud of hunger covers me completely
and I wonder at my own sanity. Am I a child

of God when I live in my addiction? When I live
in my sobriety? When I believe in Jesus? When
I confess my sins? When I eat until I pass out?

I Want To Use My Gifts

I want to use my God-given gifts to make
a difference. I want to be completely sober
and completely humble. (Bless the Children
and Angels in our midst.) Let us live honestly
and drenched completely in love.

My Struggle To Do Good

The good book says that He who has begun
a good work in me will complete a good work in
me. I shall wait patiently, then, for the more I
struggle to do good, the less I actually do.

Legal Prayer

I shall trust in the Lord with all my heart, for my
own understanding is rather skewed. I cannot think
clearly or live purely, as feelings and mirages wrap
themselves around my gentle heart. Am I under the
influence? I believe so. (The law forbids that which
is natural and of the heart: why?) I shall trust in the
Lord, then, for I cannot trust in my own, unlawful
heart.

Repentance Acknowledged

I've only wanted to be good, but the steps
I've taken to be good have been wrong—for my
goodness will not save me. Please forgive my ignorance,

world. When all existence breathes a sigh of relief after the passing of Ignorance, then perhaps we will have peace and goodness. For now, I repent passionately.

If I Were

If they were to be celebrate me, would I be any happier? If I were completely satisfied with the art of my existence, would I be any happier? If my body were as thin as a reed, would I be any happier? If the world were at peace, would I be any happier? If all of my friends and family were to know the Lord, would I be any happier? If the colors of the world wrapped themselves around me like a warm, beautiful cocoon, would I be any happier?

The Family Weeps

The child weeps. He needs his father.
The father weeps. He needs his son.
The family weeps to stay together.

Change Me

The nothingness of time causes my heart to ache. What will change the nothingness? What will reverse the apathy? Christ alone? I hesitate to place my faith in someone I cannot see. I fear failure. I fear love. Change me, great force of life and creation. Change me, that I might carry out good deeds, and bless those I see before me.

The Alcoholic

The alcoholic drinks to cool the burning fire rather than to ease the thirst. The food addict eats to fill the unfillable pit rather than to

ease the hunger. I fathom the plight of the addict. I understand the
impossible quest of the insatiable, ravenous heart.

God Calls Our Physical Bodies His Holy Temple

God calls our physical bodies His Holy Temple. For me,
this translates into: Sanctuary for the Arts. I grew up a dancer.
At the tender age of four I fell in love with ballet and everything
it represents: grace, control, balance, and expression. I fed myself
well and I got plenty of rest and exercise. My body was truly my
temple, my sanctuary, my tool, and my medium. One artist said
that *the message is the medium*. If this is true, then as dancers,
the medium is also the message.

My *message* is 'God is peace and love,' and my *medium* is art.
Or, you might say that my *message* is art, and my *medium* is
'God is peace and love.' Either way, the intent is sincere.

Art Promotes Peace

Here is my thesis and mission statement: Art promotes peace
because it profoundly and necessarily involves sharing, which
grows compassion among us. Webster's defines sharing as: *to
enjoy with others*. How wonderful!

Inspiration or Ice-spiration

I watch in awe as
they glide effortlessly
over the ice
like angels of God
on frozen water—
Jesus walked on water.
(Christ-likeness is creative!
Our lives are dancing
set to music.)
I am inspired by the

figure skaters,
for they are elegant
and strong,
walking holily
on frozen water.

What Shall I Wear?

The calmness of life is mine.
The quietness of life is mine.
All that's happened before does
not belong to me,
and all that will come
is neither mine. I accept
solemnly the failures of this
world, and of my body.
I praise jubilantly the loving
merciful God and Savior who is
so great that we cannot comprehend
his greatness! Whatever shall I
wear to heaven, to see You, my
great God and Savior?

Jewelry, Make Me Beautiful

Oh jewels of gold and glitter
and shine! Wreath my face, my
neck, my head, mine, mine!

Come and make me beautiful, that
at His return I may be sufficiently,
betrothingly, and bewilderingly
handsome and lovely!

(The natural air of my canter
and flesh is not enough—
I wish to SHINE!)

Beyond Me

The complete and utter joy
of performing envelops me
when I am on stage,
in my costume,
in my fake eyelashes,
in my red lips. The lights
embrace me and
the dark audience
entices me. I am
bigger than my body—
for the Energy which
controls me
is divine. It is
supernatural, spiritual,
magnificent!
I am beyond
my mortal self.

Blessed

How can one person
be so blessed?
My opportunities
are more beautiful
than all normal purposes
and all basic necessities.
My soul soars
at its good fortune.
My heart bursts
with satisfaction,
disbelief, and joy:
I am involved
in local theatre!

The Needs of One Person

Though the Lord

did not give me
a good singing voice,
I am blessed. Though
he did not give me
money or jewels,
I am blessed.
The dancing fills me
with physical joy
and spiritual calm,
and that is all
one person
needs.

The Call of the Stage
for Emily Bronte

Whatever our souls are made of, his
and mine are the same.
I understand his, and he understands mine.
But we remain separated, why?
Because life calls me away from him—
to the lights, the theatre, the clamor!
I am called to sing, to dance, to perform
like a cheerful wind-up doll.
I cannot rest with him.
The earthy darkness of our forged, common souls
becomes a distant, romantic ideal, and I go floating
and flying into the realms with actors, angels,
and the spirits of art and creativity!
I fly far, far away
to the splintering rafters
of the glittering,
glamorous, glorious stage.

Sign of Love

How can He
love me so much
as to give me

the experience of:
musical movement,
graceful gesture,
physical poetry,
orchestral occupation,
concave and convex
cuddlings of feet to floor:
dancing.

Love Poem to Music

Sweetness and goodness
seep out my bones,
my pores,
my feminine appendages.
I desire thee, Music,
to cover me. I want
only to move with thee,
make love to thee,
touch and comfort thee—
that no emptiness or grief
shall plague either
one of us ever again.

Sweetly and Brightly

Encourage one another, friends,
that blackness may not affect us,
hurt us, or bring us down, as it once
did. Let us uplift one another holily,
sweetly, brightly. Amen.

Plea To God

Fill me, fill me, so that all feelings of
agony and anorexia are chased ruthlessly
and mercilessly away.

Waves of Ecstasy

Waves of ecstasy wash over my brain
while I dance, entertaining you and delighting
me. My love for movement—for the extreme agile
ability and poetic possibility of the human body—is
an ocean of joy and pleasure.

Again!

Let me dance for you, Jesus!
Let my limbs be yours.
Let my torso—curved and firm—
be yours.
I've danced for you before,
Jesus, let me do it again.
Oh, let me again!

Dreams

My dreams
are the flagstones
of my habits,
my actions,
my responsibilities,
my commitments.
I go confidently
toward my dreams,
Jesus, because
I believe that
they are holy and
you are holy.
Your sweet,
perfect purity
inspires me onward!

Elements of Heaven

Holiness and serenity

wrap themselves
like comforting friends
around my cold, cold heart.
They are wonderful
friends! Without them
I am merely
aloof.

Vibrant Purple

Purple represents royalty, extravagance,
luxury. I seek to embody the vibrancy of
purple in my life, my art, my dancing.

My King

My King, let me dance for you!
I wish for nothing else! I desire
only the simplest of desires!

Always

Always I shall be yours, Jason, for your
hands shape my hands perfectly and the front
of your body shapes the back of my body perfectly.
The coming together of yourself and myself is most
conveniently and geometrically proportionate. I am
blessed. I shall always be yours.

Things which Distract Me

I am preoccupied with design, line, pattern,
symmetry, light, smoothness, and balance. I am
spectacularly concerned with shape and form and
color. I am distracted by the things of the world,

by the things which are seen with the
eyes and not with the heart.

Bank Teller Morning

The coffee at the beginning of my day
is a saving grace. It enters my mouth, falls
down inside my body; past my throat, my heart,
my intestines, and into my deep, feminine stomach.
It draws me up and vivifies me, getting me artificially
and sufficiently ready for my bank teller day.

From Jesus

The upwelling grace within me must come from
Jesus, for on my own, I am a pile of bitterness and
greed.

Inconspicuous

I look out the window at the moving cars. They
require gasoline to barrel down the streets. Each one
is a streak of muted color; drab colors mostly. We do
not travel in neon or rainbow-hued vehicles. We
wish to be inconspicuous perhaps.

Case of Old Love

I have a case of old love.
It is my precious companion,
my suitcase, my cargo.
It is dear and fragile and historic.
I carry it around with me; I cannot let it go.
I shall not. It is mine! This old, old love.

Mastery of Language

Mastery of the English language is
certainly not my place of residence, of
ownership, of license. I know only that which
I understand, and I understand only that with I like.
My mastery is quite limited, therefore.

Beautiful Hardwood Floor

Beautiful hardwood floor, how I adore thee.
Rosy and warm and smooth. like my ideals. (My
dreams and aspirations are noble and good.) I pray
to be strong and resilient like the beautiful hard-
wood floor beneath me. Amen.

Henry Ward Beecher

Henry Ward Beecher wrote that 'Gratitude is the
fairest blossom which springs from the soul.' I almost
agree with him for when I am grateful, life seems more fair.

William Shakespeare wrote, 'But thy eternal summer shall not
fade.' I almost agree with him, because the seasons of the soul
are much more significant than the seasons of the earth.

Bertrand Russell wrote, 'It is preoccupation with possession, more
than anything else that prevents men from living freely and nobly.'
I must say, I agree with him, for when I am concerned with car,
house, clothing and food I feel very trapped indeed. But when
I cast my cares on God for all provisions, I feel free!

Blue of Sky

Do you think blue is a calming color because the sky is
blue, or, do you think God make the sky blue because blue
is a calming color?

Darling Dave

His darling face compliments his darling personality
which compliments his darling hands which compliment
his darling feet which compliment his darling walk, darling
words, and darling hat upon darling head.

Jesus' Light

I am nothing without Jesus, for his light shines
within me more powerfully than anything else.
Shine, Jesus, shine!!

Honing Thought

How many poems must I write before I
am pleased with the quality of my own thoughts,
with the beauty of my own expressions? I am not sure
of the requisite number of poems, but the number of years
will probably exceed one thousand thousand.

The Precious Home

The home, the precious home,
is where the heart returns again
and again. I travel, of course, but
I am pulled homeward each time,
like a man to his wife.

The Artist's Colors

Plaid patterns dance like stars
on the papers in my artist's studio.
Pink for this, yellow for that, blue
for the sky (of course) and silver

surrounds all. Gold the home
plate. Gold the home plate.

Luminous Hope

One day my fears will
disperse completely and all
that shall remain will be my
luminous hope. Jesus, take
me to that glorious day
faster than I might
get there on
my own.

I Shall Live Courageously

I shall live courageously, Jesus,
for I know that I am fearfully and
wonderfully made. Thank you Jesus,
for knitting me together in my mother's
womb. I sing my deepest praises to Thee,
and my deepest gratitude to she.

Tiredness, My Closest Companion

Tiredness is my closest companion.
How long has it been this way? Perhaps
since forever.

The Importance of Grace

I over-exaggerate the importance of grace.
I strive to display it body and soul, but the body
limps from hunger & the soul crumbles from solitude
and surrender. Perhaps my definition of grace is skewed.

If Your grace is good and holy, Jesus, then why is mine
definitively uncomfortable and painful?

Lack of Nourishment

Over my heart is drawn a veil of hunger,
which so drastically hides the blood of life
that I cannot nourish myself or others. The
woman obedient is a sorry thing to behold.
She wants only to ease the man's questing
for beauty. But what about her own quest
for beauty? Surely, the outer self is not
as important as the inner self.

I Fully Desire Love

I fully desire love. But my yearning to create
outshines everything. The yearning which is fuller
than full, louder than loud, and bigger than big covers
all natural and unnatural appetites. Without complaining,
I live. Without affection, I live.

Creative Silence

Creative silence, creative talk.
Non-creative silence, non-creative talk.
Which is my destiny, here at the bank?

The Positive Side of Love

At the touch of love, I become calm.
I become lacking of anxiety, speed, and
the desperate need to do. At the touch of
love, the corners of my mouth curve
upward, and my heart, which

normally races, slows
sweetly down.

On the Eternal Side

On the eternal side of life is
where I reside. My dancing and
poetry do not live today. They live
forever, and I live happily with them.

Why?

Why did I have to make her feel bad?
Rather than 'Hello, how are you?' I said,
'Nice of you to show up for the meeting.'
Unkind, unnecessary, sarcastic… Lord,
help me to speak only in kindness and
necessity.

Help me to love people rather than chide
people. I wish to be your mouth and your
ears, but I speak rudely and icily! I act im-
maturely, selfishly. God, help me to change
and improve. My natural inclinations are
desperate and ridiculing. Let me not
shun love, but love love. Let me
do your work, God! Amen.

Your Perfect Brow

Upon your perfect brow
I place my trust. Like a little
star, bright and floating, I
place my trust upon
your brow.

Creative Silence

Thank you for what you give me, Lord.
This creative silence—precious and true—
is as valuable as diamonds. It is my contemplation, my dreaming, my listening to You.

Let Me Dance For Good Reason

Let me dance for good reason, Lord, not
for myself, but for You. Let me dance holily,
sweetly, lovingly, my Lord, not for myself,
but for You.

Soft, Silent Box

He lives in something I completely understand:
a bubble, a box, a foam-lined vault. He cannot hear
or see us. He wishes to, perhaps, but he cannot. The liquid
in his brain—which he voluntarily has put there— keeps him
in his soft, silent box. My bulimia, likewise, familiarized me
with this box, and so I understand.

We must love those living in soft, silent boxes. We who
are free must love those who are not.

The Social Self

Some of us enjoy the social quality of ourselves.
Some of us strive to be more social or more wonderful.
Some of us struggle to be liked or popular. My aim is not
to be who I am not, Lord, but to be who I am. Allow me Lord,
to be exactly what you've made me to be. The destined actions
and accomplishments of my life are yours and mine, Lord.
Bless this union Lord, yours and mine!

Jesus

My Lord is an example of grace and resilience. My patience is
a direct reflection of my faith in His promise to save the world. I
trust the significance of divinity, the strength of grace and purity.

Haiku

I am a crazy
artist. There is nothing I
would prefer to be.

Lovely One

What moves through your beautiful brain?
What waves do you ride upon?
What colors fill your dreams?
What skies envelop you?
What is the secret to your loveliness?
What is the zenith of your appeal?
What is the peak of your incredible, delectable charm?

A Poor State of Affairs

There is always room for improvement.
If this is the case, then I shall never be improved.
For, upon achieving one bit of betterness, a new void
of destitution will surely follow. What a pity!

Elegance of Soul

The monster inside of me
is an insatiable beast of
hunger and thirst and desire.
Yearning for patience!

Yearning for solemnity!
Yearning for calmness!
The elegance of my soul
is untapped and
unreachable.
I cannot find it.

Why I Dance

For all that has come before and all that is yet to come,
I dance. For the desires inside of me, I dance. For beauty of
love and holiness, I dance. For smoothness of floor, hardness
of muscle, and flexibility of skin, I dance. *God sent his only
begotten son into the world, that we might live through him.*
(1 John 4:9) May our lives be beautiful stories of grace,
strength, and passion.

My Love

I will not see his handsome, truthful face today
for my love lives far away, in a land of barking dogs
and yellow cars that do not stop. Will he sleep the day
through or dance or smoke or sing or play? My love is a
poet of fragility and masculinity, of boldness and strength.
I have nothing but respect and admiration for my love, but
I do not have face time.

Dream Sweet

A dream is a dream is a dream.
A rose by any other name
would smell as sweet.
Dream sweet, my lovely rose,
dream sweet!

The Murderous Beach of Love

The murderous beach of love
is a place of desire and torment.
How can my former lover strut around
so nakedly, so elegantly, so ignorant-ly of me?
I, in my turtle-necked swimsuit; in my layers
and layers of self-defense.
How can I sit here, basking in the warmth
of this yellow, yellow sun,
all wanting, wanting?
Bring me calm, dear waves of blue sweet salt,
bring me calm.
Jesus, reel me in.
Jesus, reel me in.

Life Is A Beautiful Flower

I wasted so much time because I thought I was too fat,
too heavy, too fleshy. The extra weight prevented me from
doing what I love. What a travesty. What a hearbreak. What a
complete and utter detriment to my dancing soul. I sat in a chair
because I was afraid of not having the perfect body. And so, not
only my limbs suffered, but my mind, heart, strength, creativity,
spirituality, growth, productivity, and expression suffered. I
robbed myself, and perhaps my fellow dancers, of art,
opportunity and joy simply because the numbers
on the scale did not say what I wanted
them to say. I regret my decade
of stillness. This is the *only*
regret I have known.

Life is a beautiful flower that blooms
in unplanned and unprecedented directions.

I urge you, friends, do not let your understanding
of the situation prevent you from participating *in* the
situation. If the Lord calls you to dance, then dance with
all of your might, regardless of the numbers on the scale.

Art Community Center Vision

We are a community center for artists. We offer free space to artists: free rehearsal space, free exhibit space, free class space, free performance space. The only thing we ask for is 20% of all sales. This money helps to keep the center going. We also gratefully accept financial donations and contributions from friends and supporters.

We are a cooperative project. We are open Thursday through Sunday, 11-6pm. The beauty of Bucks County deeply inspires us and we wish to give back to the community. Please email us anytime at danceofmyhands@aol.com. We would love to hear from you! (This is one of my many visions.)

One Wish

I do not wish to be something I am not.
I do not wish to be insincere in ANY WAY.
Let the love and truth of the Lord run
throuuuuuuuuuugh my body
and out my eyes,
my fingertips,
my toetips,
my hairtips.
Let the grace of Jesus be
sweetly expressed and
beautifully demonstrated by
anything I might do or want
or have or be.
Let all that comes into my life
be under the complete influence
of Jesus Christ.
If honesty is humility, then
the walk of my life—
as described above—
shall be very humble indeed.

With sincerity and love,

Melanie Monterey Eyth
danceofmyhands@aol.com

www.ingramcontent.com/pod-product-compliance
Lightning Source LLC
LaVergne TN
LVHW091319080426
835510LV00007B/567